Jesus beca̲ ̲̲̲̲̲̲̲̲̲̲̲̲̲̲̲̲̲ ̲̲̲̲̲̲̲̲̲̲̲̲̲̲̲̲̲nicate
the gospel ι ̲̲̲̲̲̲̲̲̲̲̲̲̲̲̲̲̲ ̲̲e way. We
too must sta̲ ̲̲̲̲̲̲̲̲̲̲̲̲̲̲̲̲̲ ̲̲es (or slippers)
to effectively ι ̲̲̲̲̲̲̲̲̲̲̲̲̲̲̲̲̲.e the gospel to our
Japanese neighbι ̲̲̲̲̲̲̲̲this book is a very helpful
tool to have in your bag.

TONY SCHMIDT
Former OMF missionary to Japan,
now serving Japanese people in Canada

A must read for any Christian who seeks better
communication with any Japanese. This booklet
will give you a good understanding of why
Japanese people think and act as they do, and
offer practical tips on how to move forward.

YOSHIE YOKOYAMA
OMF Returnee Focus Japan Country Leader;
Minister of Shiki Church (UCCJ), Greater Tokyo, Japan

This is a really helpful booklet for someone wishing to better understand the worldview of a Japanese friend or contact and how to show them the love of Christ more effectively. Understanding more about where your friend is coming from, along with the many practical ideas offered in this booklet will, as you pray, help you connect with them and share Jesus' message of the good news of the kingdom and forgiven life in the family of God in a way they will more easily grasp. I highly recommend this short and readable booklet.

SELVAN ANKETELL
Director, Mission for Japan Christian Link, UK

This guide will be a very useful resource for anyone wanting to engage with Japanese people. It gives rich insights into Japan's history and culture alongside lots of practical tips for befriending, witnessing to and discipling those from a very different culture to our own. The questions it raises could also well be good pointers to engaging with other nationalities.

SUE BURT
Head of Returnee Ministry, Friends International

SHARING
YOUR
FAITH
WITH YOUR
JAPANESE
NEIGHBOUR

CHRISTIAN
FOCUS

Copyright © OMF International 2025

paperback ISBN 978-1-5271-1186-8
ebook ISBN 978-1-5271-1259-9

10 9 8 7 6 5 4 3 2 1

Published in 2025
by
Christian Focus Publications Ltd,
Geanies House, Fearn, Ross-shire,
IV20 1TW, Great Britain.
www.christianfocus.com

Cover design by Pete Barnsley (CreativeHoot.com)

Printed and bound by
Bell & Bain, Glasgow

Contents

Foreword

In today's complex modern society, mission work is becoming increasingly diverse. As the world becomes more globalized, the work of missions is not only preaching the gospel in fields abroad. Many Japanese people, while overseas for reasons such as study, work and international marriage, have been exposed to the gospel, encountered Jesus Christ, and had their lives changed.

According to one study, Japanese people are thirty times more likely to be saved abroad than in Japan. There are many possible factors behind this, but it may be that when someone leaves their home country and enters a new place with a different culture and language, they are freed from certain things that previously restricted them. In such circumstances, it occurs to them to think about their lives, which can result in sensing and facing up to the existence of the Almighty – maybe for the very first time. Many Japanese people, from various backgrounds, are coming to experience new life in Jesus and invariably someone has brought them the good news. In many cases, they see the radiance of Christ at work in the person who tells them of Him – and are touched by their love. Through this they come to know God's truth and receive the grace and blessings of salvation. I too was saved in that way – in America – and now I am preaching the gospel in England.

The Japanese are said to be one of the most difficult people in the world to evangelise. I think there are a variety of reasons for this, but they all stem from Japan's particular history, culture, and customs. In this book, based on the valuable experiences of OMF missionaries over the years, there is a wealth of knowledge compiled in an easy-to-understand manner that's useful for reaching out to Japanese people. While respecting the culture and ways of thinking that Japanese people value, we hope you will learn how to convey God's truth and love to their hearts and lead as many as possible to Christ. Many people around the world with a burden for the Japanese have been ministering to them. Together may we pray and work for the salvation of this special people whom the Lord loves so much.

*Pastor **Katsutoshi Shimizu***
South London Japanese Christian Church

Preface

It just started from a cup of tea. The funny thing is that she was the only person I met in England who didn't like tea. That was surprising for me because I'd thought that everyone in the UK loved tea. So, while she drank soda and I had tea, we regularly met on Friday afternoons to share what we were doing and study the Bible together. While I was in the UK there were several times when people shared the gospel with me, but I found it particularly helpful to have a one-to-one Bible study partner. We read through the Gospel of Mark; this was my first experience of reading the Bible chapter by chapter. My friend also helped me with some English words because it was a struggle to read the Bible in a foreign language. Furthermore, even though it was her first time doing a one-to-one Bible study with a Japanese person, I felt very encouraged that she was trying to do her best to help me. (If my friend had known about this booklet, she would have got hold of a copy!) As we read the Bible verse by verse, she asked me if I had any questions or not. Step by step, I was able to listen to God's Word and understand the real meaning of Christian faith.

This booklet gives many tips on how to reach out to Japanese people and share the love of Jesus, whether you are meeting with a group or an individual. It will help you to understand their background, such as their history, religious views and characteristics of their nationality. It is important to have some understanding of these things, in order to reach out, but also so that you can understand your Japanese friend more deeply and build a closer relationship.

Looking back on my experience, I think there are quite a lot of Japanese people who are waiting for someone to reach out and share the gospel with them. Japanese people tend to be shy and not many will directly ask you to share the gospel with them. However, they might admit to you privately that they are actually interested in reading the Bible and finding out about Christianity. Before I became a Christian, I thought Christianity was a 'Western religion' and part of 'Western culture' and in order to understand British culture I thought it was essential to learn about Christianity. I think many Japanese people have a similar idea and it is quite common for them to have an interest in Christianity, especially if they like history, art, music, literature and so on. In my case, I had some experience of going to church and reading the Bible as I'd graduated from a Christian University. (There are quite a lot of Christian schools and universities in Japan, which were mostly founded by missionaries in the past.) However, the majority of Japanese people have no experience of going to church or encountering the Bible. You might be the first ever person to share the gospel with them!

Reaching out to Japanese people might feel challenging at first but this booklet will assist you to love and share the gospel with your friend. Even if you feel there's little you can do, that is still part of God's work. You never know what God will do in your friend's life. The apostle Paul said, 'I planted the seed, Apollos watered it, but God has been making it grow' (1 Cor. 3:6). God has arranged things so that each one of us has a part to play in his wonderful plan. So please don't hesitate to take a step forward. This booklet will be the best partner for you!

Anna Yamamura is a Japanese primary school teacher who came to know Jesus while studying abroad. After her studies, and being baptized, she returned to Japan where she has since gotten involved in church life.

CHAPTER ONE

A Deeper Look at Japan

A Brief Outline of Japan's History

Like all nations, Japan's past deeply affects the identity of its people today. Understanding a few historical points will be helpful in building your friendship.

An Island Nation

Japan's history has given rise to a strongly defined national psyche. Ancient mythology says Japan was created by the kami (gods) as a sacred land to be ruled by a sacred emperor who was a descendant of the supreme kami, the sun goddess Amaterasu. Originally much of Japan was inhabited by the aboriginal Ainu people, but they were driven out as other groups came in from Korea, China and the southern Japanese islands. A tiny number of Ainu still live in parts of the northern island of Hokkaido. Their appearance is different from the vast majority of Japanese people.

After considerable Chinese influence around A.D. 400–900 a distinctive Japanese culture emerged followed by the rise of the military samurai class and the rule of the shoguns in the late twelfth century.[1] During a period of over 100 years of civil war, the first Europeans (Portuguese) set foot in Japan with the first Christian missionary, Francis Xavier arriving in 1549. After the Tokugawa family took power as shoguns, they closed Japan off from the rest of the world in 1639. Christianity was forbidden and all but eradicated. The shoguns, ruling supposedly in the emperor's name, maintained a strong centralized feudal structure and the status distinctions between the samurai, merchants, artisans and peasants were enforced.

After more than 200 years of isolation, Japan reluctantly reopened to the West when Commodore Perry of the US navy arrived in 1853. The resulting trade and international relations set in motion a chain of events that ultimately ended the rule of the shoguns. The Meiji Restoration in 1868, named after the new emperor, restored imperial rule to Japan. Shinto became the state religion emphasising the emperor as a divine

---

1 Shoguns were hereditary commanders-in-chief in feudal Japan from 1192–1867.

being – though the ban on Christianity was also lifted. From then on, Japan made tremendous efforts to 'catch up' with the West and rapid change occurred in every aspect of national life. This resulted in a growing national confidence and the beginnings of an empire overseas.

After a brief spell of growth in democratic institutions, the far right became increasingly powerful and Japan came under military leadership in the 1930s. The invasion of China in 1937 eventually brought Japan into World War II with the attack on Pearl Harbour in December 1941.[2] After the dropping of two atomic bombs Japan was finally defeated in 1945. The consequent occupation (primarily American) brought about significant change starting with a new constitution in which the right to wage war was renounced and full religious freedom granted. The next forty years saw increasing westernization, the growth of new religious sects and the so-called 'economic miracle' which was fuelled by high exports and technological developments. However, from the 1990s economic growth slowed down considerably and other significant challenges began to emerge such as a rapidly ageing population and social isolation. At the same time Japanese cuisine and pop culture (such

---

2 Mitsou Fuchida led the first wave of the Japanese attack on Pearl Harbour. He later became a Christian after the war and shared his testimony in his autobiography *From Pearl Harbour to Calvary*, available at the time of writing as an ebook.

as manga and anime) has become popular around the world. Furthermore, the economy remains the third largest in the world (as of June 2022).

One People

The Japanese are a homogeneous people. With few exceptions, they have a common ancestry, appearance, and culture throughout the four islands. They consider uniformity a good thing and view non-conformity as a threat to social harmony. The Japanese have a proverb which says, 'the nail that sticks up should be hammered down'.

Japanese Attitudes Toward Foreigners

The Japanese have been borrowing from other nations for centuries. Much of their language and culture has been borrowed from China. Buddhism, one of their major religions, came from India via China and then Korea. The first contact with Europe led to Portuguese and Dutch influence on language, food and customs. Politically, the first constitution of 1889 was greatly impacted by that of Germany. Since World War II it has been very much American culture that has left its mark in many ways.

Many Japanese people hold two attitudes simultaneously: a healthy curiosity in foreign things and a strong national pride. As you explain about your country's way of doing things, take a genuine interest in the Japanese culture and show respect for it and for its people.

Christianity is Not New

Christianity is not a recent import to Japan. Francis Xavier (1506–52) brought Roman Catholicism to Japan in 1549 and for over sixty years there was significant church growth, with feudal lords and their people converting to Christianity. But then various social and political factors led to severe persecution. During the Tokugawa Shogunate era, Christianity was forbidden. Missionaries were expelled and thousands of Christians were martyred. (This was portrayed very starkly in the 2016 film *Silence*, based on the book by Shusaku Endo.)

Over 200 years later Japan opened up to the West again and not long afterwards Christianity was tolerated again. In fact, as Emperor Meiji (1868–1912) encouraged people to adopt Western culture, Christianity and its influence began to spread. Some Japanese people were sent overseas to study and to return with the necessary skills to educate others. Quite a few also returned with the gospel. Several of Japan's public figures of this period took a clear stand for Christ.

Some Christians from this era whose names will be familiar to many Japanese today are Jo Niijima, who started Doshisha, a famous university in Kyoto; Inazo Nitobe, who was an Under-Secretary General of the League of Nations and was previously pictured on the 5000 yen bill; Kanzo Uchimura, who was a leading journalist and writer; and Umeko Tsuda, who founded

Tsuda University for women in Tokyo. She is due to be featured on new Japanese banknotes issued in 2024.

"What About the War?"

During the Second World War, Christians were often suspected of being spies from the West. Pressure was brought on them to honour the Emperor and support the war effort. Most did; and many of those who refused were imprisoned. Since 1945, the Japanese have been educated with a strong anti-war ethos, although there has been a vigorous campaign to adjust the peaceful 'self-defence-only' constitution which was adopted after the war. There has also been a concerted campaign by some to ensure that young Japanese people are taught to be proud of their history, no matter what. This is usually more influential than any thoughts of accepting a portion of blame for the war; the invasions in China and Southeast Asia and the attack on Pearl Harbour are often played down.

Some Japanese people are sensitive and perhaps embarrassed about this topic, perhaps aware of different views of history and wanting to avoid any open disagreement about it. Sensitivity and caution is advised when talking about it. If the topic arises, asking questions about what your Japanese friend thinks, or has studied about, may well be a good way forward. You could perhaps try asking about your friend's parents or grandparents experience of wartime Japan.

Snapshot: Visiting a museum in Singapore about the Second World War with his father, a pastor, a ten-year-old Japanese boy, Jun, felt shock and horror seeing some of the actions of the Japanese soldiers at the time. As he left the museum he said to his dad: 'I don't want to be Japanese'. But seeing the love shown to his family by his hosts during their visit he was able to grow deeper in his appreciation of forgiveness as well as his understanding of the past.

Whatever country we come from, there are things in our history to be ashamed of. As Christians, we can learn to face up to the truth of this and avoid judging others. God knows the worst about us all – both as individuals and as nations. Yet he is a God who, in love, is always ready to forgive.

Japanese Attitudes to Religion

In general, Japanese people are not opposed to religion per se, nor are they cynical about religion, but many would be suspicious of what they might consider to be enthusiastic religious devotion. Older generations and those living in more rural areas tend to be more conservative than younger people and those living in the cities, as they have more opportunities to participate in their local and traditional religions. Many Japanese people are nervous about cults. In 1995 the doomsday cult, Aum Shinrikyo, carried out a deadly sarin gas attack on the Tokyo subway. More recently there have also been many other cults proselytizing on university campuses. Since the assassination of former Prime Minister Shinzo Abe in 2022, there has been intense scrutiny of the Unification Church and other so-called 'Christian' cults which are seen as controlling and detrimental to family life. As the great majority of Japanese people don't know the difference between these cults and orthodox Christian churches, this has increased hesitation among many to trust Christian groups and organisations.

When considering different religions, Japanese people often use the illustration of there being several paths up a mountain, all leading to the top. On Mount Fuji there are five such paths. So there may be different religions, but they all lead to the same end. Consequently, most Japanese people are pluralistic and willing to follow several religions at the same time. They may be willing to consider a new religion as an extra belief in the sense of an extra insurance policy – something which might be useful. Many 'new religions' (various sects which have arisen in the past century are often syncretistic and incorporate Shinto, Buddhist or even Christian elements) arising in Japan take advantage of this attitude and encourage people to take part and experience the blessings without necessarily explaining what doctrine the person is meant to believe.

Religion in Japan: Shinto, Buddhism

How do ancestor worship and emperor worship mix with Confucian ethics in Japan's modern, materialist society? Is my Japanese friend Shinto or Buddhist, a mixture or something else?

Snapshot: After leaving the hot spring bath, my friend Koji leaves a bottle of juice at the base of a beautiful old tree, and then closes his eyes for a moment, holding his hands together. 'We believe in the spirit of the tree' he says. 'What is it like? How did it get there?' I ask. Koji is amused by my question and smiles, but can't give an answer.

The Japanese Agency for Cultural Affairs figures from 2022 indicate that 66 percent of Japanese people adhere to a Buddhist faith of some kind. At the same time, just under 70 percent are adherents of Shinto, the traditional Japanese animistic religion of 'an uncountable myriad of gods'. So it is likely that a Japanese person you meet will take part in both Buddhist and Shinto activities, but may well not have any firmly held beliefs connected with them.

Most Japanese adherents of Buddhism or Shinto do not attend weekly meetings. They simply follow various ceremonies and customs of the religions. Many homes have both a Shinto god-shelf and a Buddhist family altar. Ceremonies to do with life and local festivals are normally

Shinto, whereas nearly 80 percent of funerals are conducted according to elaborate Buddhist rites. A significant part of the practices is to pray when visiting temples or shrines – prayers for good health, good luck or success in exams – but often those who do so don't think in precise terms about who or what they are praying to.

Aside from Buddhist or Shinto priests and a small proportion of particularly keen adherents, usually only those who belong to smaller sects or to the new religions are likely to be definite in their beliefs. Another thing to bear in mind is that around fifty percent of Japanese couples who get married do so in a Christian ceremony – certainly far more than the proportion of Japanese people considering themselves to be Christians! Generally, these weddings are arranged by hotels, often in purpose-built hotel chapels, who call in a pastor or missionary to perform the service. Many simply employ hotel staff, or any westerner, regardless of their religious beliefs, to act the part.

Bearing all this in mind, it is best to ask about the practices and beliefs that your friend follows with both sensitivity and interest. However, it may help you in your discussions with your friend to know a little about Shinto and Buddhism in Japan in general.

Shinto
Shinto is indigenous to Japan. It is an animistic religion based on the worship of gods and

goddesses in various aspects of nature. The myth of Japan's creation through the sun goddess Amaterasu forms part of their Shinto belief. The religious rites broadcast worldwide during the accession of the emperor in 2019 were Shinto and the Emperor Cult is part of the state Shinto religion.

Shinto is the origin of most Japanese festivals, when excited crowds will be seen pushing, pulling or carrying portable shrines. At New Year, crowds flock to their local Shinto shrine to pray for good luck in the coming year.

> **Snapshot:** 'Why don't we visit that shrine to pray for good luck in your Japanese exam?', Sayaka asks as we pass a Shinto shrine on our walk. 'Thanks, but I only pray to my own God, the Christian God' I say. Sayaka is surprised: 'Aren't gods similar? I also pray in Buddhist ceremonies at a funeral, and when I get married I want to have a Christian wedding, so I guess I'll pray to that god then'.

Family rites of passage, with the usual exception of funerals, will almost certainly have a Shinto element to them. A baby is dressed up in a kimono and has a photograph taken when it is 100 days old and may also be taken along to the shrine for a blessing. When boys are three and five years old, and girls are three and seven, they are taken to the shrine in traditional dress, where prayers of gratitude are offered for their growth so far, and petitions made for their future health and success. A traditional Japanese wedding is held in accordance with Shinto rites, the bride and groom dressed in a traditional kimono.

When a new house or factory is to be built, a 'ground breaking' ceremony is normally conducted by the Shinto priests, placating the spirits disturbed by the building activity. A talisman is placed in the roof beams for the protection of the builders and the future residents of the house from bad luck. Construction workers are still usually insistent on such a ceremony being performed.

In many houses there will be a small shelf about head height on the wall of the living room. This is a Shinto god-shelf. It is little used throughout the year, but on New Year's Eve, it will be carefully cleaned, and new offerings of rice cakes and perhaps a sprig of pine will be placed on it for good luck in the coming year. More dedicated families may clap and bow to the god-shelf at other times too.

Buddhism

The roots of Buddhism in Japan are deep and many Japanese would identify themselves as Buddhist. Others would think of Buddhism as their 'family religion', though personally identifying as 'non-religious'.

Buddhism first entered Japan around A.D. 550 from Korea. In the seventh and early eighth centuries, several prominent Buddhist schools were opened by the Chinese. During this time Buddhism was promoted as the state religion, and official monasteries were established in every province. It was not until this time that Buddhism really became established in Japan.

A variety of Buddhist denominations then developed. In the early ninth century two new Buddhist sects were introduced, and in the early twelfth century Zen Buddhism arrived, again from China, and was adopted by the dominant military class. Around the same time the popular Nichiren and Pure Land Buddhism sects emerged from within Japan itself, though influenced by writings emanating from China.

The Tokugawa Government (1603–1867) worked to restrict and regulate religious activity. As part of this they nevertheless used Buddhism and its network of temples to help eradicate Christianity. However, after the Meiji Restoration in 1868, the government sought to establish Shinto as the national religion, and many Buddhist temples were disestablished.

Though the ascetic influence of Zen Buddhism in Japanese culture may be seen in the discipline of the tea ceremony, the simplicity of flower arrangement, and the stark beauty of the temple garden, most ordinary Japanese people do not feel the impact of Buddhism on their lives until there is a death in the family.

It is said that nearly 90 percent of funerals in Japan are presided over by a Buddhist priest. As many as five separate ceremonies may be conducted, though many people in recent times are now choosing smaller scale, simpler ceremonies. The reason for the extravagant ceremonies was a desire to revere, and provide consolation for, the spirit of the deceased. There can be the unspoken fear, especially where there has been a violent or unexpected death, that the spirit may return and bring bad luck on the family. Offerings of flowers, food and drink for the repose of the spirit of the deceased are made at the funeral, and on the family altar which is in the main room in-house.

Snapshot: 'I think father would have wanted a Christian funeral, as he was attending church with mother most weeks for the last few years,' Megumi suggested to her brother.

'Nonsense, we need to do a proper funeral – what would our family say if we did such a thing. And anyway, we need to lay him to rest in the family grave, and that is Buddhist.'

'But it's nearly $10,000 dollars for the full Buddhist funeral rites', Megumi thought to herself.

The Buddhist family altar is a large ornate cabinet normally kept in the home of the eldest son in each generation, though it is often tended by his wife. A photograph of each deceased family member will be placed on the altar, along with a piece of wood on which a priest has inscribed the deceased's new name. Traditionally there would be a feeling that the spirits of the ancestors protect the family and are involved in family affairs. Any major family events will be reported to the ancestors at the family altar.

Snapshot: 'Welcome to our home – it's wonderful to have you come to stay, and to meet baby Mary too,' says Naoko as she takes our daughter in her arms, 'I'll just go and introduce her to our family'.

As she says this, she takes Mary before we can do anything and presents her before the Buddhist family altar. 'Look this is Mary, she's come to stay with us for a few days with her parents', she excitedly announces in front of the altar.

On the anniversary of a death up to the thirty-third or sometimes even the fiftieth, and particularly on special anniversaries such as the third and seventh, the priest may visit the family altar. Prayers will be offered and *sutras* are recited.[3] Such occasions are often used for family reunions.

Confucian teachings about respect for elders blend with Buddhist customs to make it very important that all the family is involved in the

---

3 A sutra is a section of Buddhist holy writings.

family worship. This is especially true for the eldest son, whose duty it will be to carry on the veneration of the ancestors when he is head of the family.

Other Religions and Philosophies

Confucianism

Originally from China, Confucianism is usually seen as a system of social and ethical philosophy, rather than a religion. Its main effect in Japan is the emphasis on loyalty, respect for elders, and the high value it places on family and filial responsibilities. Some of these values have biblical support but, when conflated with and subordinated to the emperor cult, Confucianism, with its supreme emphasis on loyalty, was one of the influences that led to the militaristic excesses of the Second World War. Confucian thinking also contributes to the company loyalty work ethic of modern Japanese business and to the high value placed on relationships within Japanese culture. It continues to have a strong, but mostly subconscious, influence on Japanese life today.

Ancestor Veneration

This is the practice of honouring and venerating deceased ancestors. Traditionally, offerings of food and, in some parts of Japan, money, will be made to the ancestors. If these rituals are not followed, it is sometimes thought that ancestors will bring misfortune on the remaining family members. It could also bring shame on the family if rituals are not performed properly.

Many of those involved feel bound by familial duty and customs to continue worshipping their ancestors, even if they personally do not want to do so. Though your Japanese friend may be keen to worship God, they are likely to feel pressure to continue the tradition of worshipping at the family altar on returning to Japan, especially since such a high value is placed on conformity. Japanese people coming to Christ usually know intuitively that, as a Christian, they would have to stop practicing ancestor veneration and this can be a stumbling block for them. It is good to remember that in the Old Testament we see that the Jewish people highly value their ancestors, but never worshipped them. Their proper worship was to be to the one true living God.

There have been some great stories of how new Christians have made a clean break with family traditions, and we should take encouragement from them. One Japanese man, a first born son, asked his father to transfer his rights in the inheritance to his brother, since he would not continue the family's worship of ancestors. In God's time, this man's father and brother also became Christians, and the man and his brother are now pastors in Japan. Getting a younger brother to take over the family responsibilities is a way many older sons have freed themselves in a socially acceptable way to become Christians.

But they are not all success stories. Another man, studying in Britain, became friends with a Christian in his hall of residence. At times the Japanese man seemed very close to believing in Christ, but he refused to be baptized, because he knew that he would have to renounce his duties as first born son to worship at the family god-shelf. He could not make the break.

Often spiritual warfare is especially intense in those who have been practicing ancestor worship. Encourage your friend first to believe in Jesus, and then to trust the Holy Spirit to help in overcoming the obstacles. We cannot ignore the difficulties, but we must not let them put individuals off deciding.

Pray that God would help your friend to understand the issue from Scripture – it is vital that they get their conviction from the Lord himself, rather than feeling obliged to comply with our perceived demands or agree with our interpretation. Pray above all that God would grant the power to renounce ancestor veneration and to acknowledge the lordship of Christ.

Cults and New Religions

There are many cults in Japan. Several 'Christian' cults, such as Mormonism, Jehovah's Witnesses, and the Unification Church ('Moonies') have all taken root. In the minds of many Japanese people, they are often indistinguishable from biblical Christianity. There are also several cults unique to Japan. These often focus on enthusiastic, ecstatic worship and offer healing or other supernatural powers.

Most of the cults attract followers from all traditional religions, and often have a charismatic leader. The proliferation of these cults reflects the spiritual hunger of those who have felt dissatisfied with traditional expressions of religion. A reaction against this over-enthusiastic religious expression may cause many people to reject, or be wary of, all kinds of 'enthusiastic' religion, including evangelical Christianity.

There is usually no conflict for the Japanese person in adhering to a plethora of religions simultaneously, so many new religions result from deviations and amalgamations of existing religions. Many are considered controversial by the mainstream press and the public.

Examples of Shinto related New Religions

- The Religion of the Divine Wisdom (*Tenrikyo*) was founded in the early nineteenth century by Miki Nakayama. Beginning with a series of reported revelations and healings, it formed its own sacred writings, constructed its own sacred city named Tenri, and developed a sacred dance and style of worship.

- Dancing Religion (*Odoru Shokyo or Tensho Kotai Jingu Kyo*) was founded by Sayo Kitamura, who believed that a *kami* (the Japanese word for the objects of worship in the Shinto faith) was speaking through her abdomen. The revelations of this *kami* formed the religion's teachings. The revelations included different names for the goddess Amaterasu and *Ise Shrine*.

- The House of Growth (*Seicho no Ie*), founded by Masaharu Taniguchi, claims to overcome disease and suffering through its teachings.

Examples of Buddhist related New Religions

- Several new movements have been established based on the Lotus Sutra.[4] Reiyukai, for example, started a movement that is now represented by a substantial meeting place in Tokyo. Rissho Koseikai, which came out of Reiyukai, is larger. Many other smaller groups have been established related to this one.

- Soka Gakkai ("Value-Creation Society") also places great emphasis on the study of the Lotus Sutra and has around 12 million members worldwide. It was founded in 1930 as a lay movement connected to the Nichiren Shoshu monastic sect. There is a strong sense of community and caring for members, and they are organized in local chapters with a definite structure and clear lines of accountability. In 1964 president Daisaku

---

4 Compiled in the first century by the council of the newly founded Mahayana Buddhist sect. The Sutra is reported to be a discourse delivered by Shakyamuni (Gautama Buddha) himself.

Ikeda formed *Komeito,* a new political party which has grown to be very influential. Although now formally separated from Soka Gakkai there are still close links. Soka Gakkai used to be known for being very militant and aggressive but in recent years has become much more peaceable.

- Kofuku no Kagaku (literally 'Happiness Science') has grown extremely rapidly since its start in 1986, now having offices worldwide. The leader, Ryuho Okawa, claimed to be the current incarnation of a supreme being.

CHAPTER TWO

Becoming a Friend

Perhaps you're reading this because you've met some Japanese people in your local area, at a church or international welcome event, at an English class, or in your school or office. Or maybe you're aware that there are Japanese people living and working nearby, and you want to reach out and befriend them.

Many Japanese people want to be friends with those from other nations. As an island nation, Japan has been learning foreign ways and borrowing what it has thought to be helpful for centuries. Some of these have been mentioned already, like the political system, economics and the white wedding dress. Even the language is filled with borrowed foreign words, especially from English. The Japanese have a natural curiosity about other parts of the world and are eager to learn from other cultures.

Those venturing overseas are likely to be particularly interested in other cultures and are probably just waiting for someone to reach out to them. Japanese students are often keen to meet local students but find it difficult to build relationships with anyone apart from other overseas students. Those working may find it hard to build relationships with people other than fellow Japanese employees.

Sometimes when making an invitation, a Japanese person may be genuinely very eager to take you up on an offer to meet. Sometimes they seem nervous and want to be sure that it is a genuine offer. Sometimes they may be keen to meet but not want to express it too obviously, appearing to be cautious, when they are in fact quite eager to say yes. And sometimes they may express positive interest to be friendly, but not really be able or willing to meet. Be patient, warm, relaxed and continue to be welcoming and friendly!

This desire for friendship though, is often not expressed in the same ways as in Western culture. Most Japanese living overseas would probably think it forward or presumptuous to take the initiative in friendship. They are particularly aware of being outsiders, especially in their first few months away from home. So be ready to make the first move – and keep at it! Perhaps you could invite them to join in with a club or group activity at your school or work. Or simply offer to go for a coffee or a meal. If there are some local points of interest, you could ask if they'd be interested to visit them together.

Social Pressures

The average Japanese person feels social pressures much more intensely than the average Westerner. In showing a lot of concern and hospitality to a Japanese person, you might possibly make them feel like they owe you something, and they could feel the need to reciprocate. The 'obligation to return favours' is strongly felt in Japanese culture.

Many Japanese students enjoy free meals or activities if these are provided to them as a group and are described as a 'student meal' or a 'student party'. But because of the sense of obligation some may not feel comfortable to receive anything from you for free. They may want to repay you by giving a gift, or to contribute in some way to maintain an equal relationship with you. For example, if you invite Japanese people to your home, they will probably want to bring some food with them to share or a gift for the host. Or some Japanese people may send you a parcel as a thank you gift after they return to Japan. They might also feel more at ease if they can pay a fee for organized groups such as toddler groups, English classes and so on.

'Saving face' is a related idea of avoiding embarrassment arising out of doing something wrong and is also an important aspect of Japanese relationships. This is not selfish pride, but a concern for both parties. So Japanese friends will be as keen to save you from embarrassment as they will be to keep their own dignity. It would be good for you to try to keep the same perspective. Always treat your friend with respect. It is probably best to avoid joking in a sarcastic way, even if you are 'just kidding'. While this may feel a natural part of friendships for you, a Japanese person may not appreciate this.

Family Ties

Family ties in Japan are generally stronger than in the West. Making friends with a Japanese person may mean that you are beginning a friendship with their whole family. If family members come over to visit from Japan, show an interest and even hospitality, if you can. You could send a Christmas card or a New Year card to them in Japan. Learn all you can about the family and pray for them as well as for your friend.

Politeness and Friendship

Japan is a 'vertical society'. This means people define their identity by those above or below them in social status. That status itself may be determined by age, wealth, education, occupation, and family connections.

The society is so stratified that this affects how Japanese people speak to each other in their own language, including how to address each other. They constantly monitor their audience and change the pronoun forms and verb endings, depending on whether they are speaking to someone on the same level, or speaking 'up' to someone of higher status or 'down' to someone of lower status. So all relationships are vertically-orientated, including friendships.

In the West, people relate very differently. Neither partner in a friendship is concerned so much about status, and we relate on more equal terms. Japanese people often have a good awareness of these differences and are eager to act according to the local norms. If this seems to be the case, the best way to love them would be to complement, encourage and help them in doing so.

Nevertheless, there are some practical steps which should ease the forming of friendships:

Learn how to pronounce your friend's name. Clarify which is the 'given' (first) name, and which is the surname. Don't be hesitant to check on pronunciation, and practice how to say it better.

Of course, we will always want to show respect to people we meet. Japanese society is one where this is especially noticed and is felt to be particularly important. Check if they're happy for you to use their first name. In Japan, it is unusual to use first names but most people know that it's different in the West.

Business cards are still used very widely in Japan, partly because it is important to know how to write a person's name, and partly to get a feel for their social status to address them properly. Japanese acquaintances may give you their card, and if they do, treat it with respect and offer yours in return if you have one. Or you can take the initiative and offer yours first. The gesture will be appreciated.

Today, in informal situations and for younger people, it is more common to simply exchange phone numbers or connect via LINE, Instagram, and other social media.

From Honeymoon to Reality

People coming to live in a foreign country typically go through a 'honeymoon period' at the start of their stay in the West. During this time, they will focus on the positive aspects of Western life: perhaps the less crowded cities and, in some countries, the sense of history and the accessibility of travelling to new places. Or perhaps they are enjoying the relaxed atmosphere in classes and the lack of pressure to conform to society's expectations. When you hear remarks along these lines, it can be good to engage them on what things they like or miss about Japan. You could respond that Japan has good points not found in many countries in the Western world, such as a strong sense of family, commitment to study and good public transport that runs on time.

This 'honeymoon period' will often be followed by a time of increasing disillusionment with Western culture. Listen to your friend's criticisms of life here without interrupting or defending your country. You can agree with justified criticisms. Defence of your own country, even if motivated only by a desire to help your friend enjoy their stay, may reinforce negative attitudes. Asking your friend about things which they find hard will give them permission to share openly about any struggles they're having.

Gradually, your Japanese friend will gain a more balanced perspective and be able to see both good and bad points of the Western way of life. This is when friendship can best develop.

How to Make Friends[1]

No one can tell you a foolproof way of how to make friends with Japanese people, but here are some practical tips that may help:

- Plan something specific and let your friend know exactly what it is. In Japan, social contacts are usually highly structured, especially at the outset.

- Go on an outing. Japanese people usually have a genuine fascination with the world, and they love to travel. Day trips to local areas of interest are often a good idea.

---

1 See also the Appendix: Ten Ways to Build Relationship

- Introduce them to your own traditions – if you're Scottish, then explain what a Burns supper is and introduce them to haggis and neaps! If you're American, invite them to your Thanksgiving dinner. Take them blackberry-picking in the autumn or invite them to a cultural celebration.

- Soccer and baseball are very popular in Japan, and many Japanese people will support a team. For many visitors an invitation to watch a game together could be something they really appreciate.

- Show them photos of your family and places you have been and ask to see theirs.

- Go to a sports or leisure centre together and arrange a friendly match of tennis or squash, a round of golf, a swim, or perhaps aerobics, badminton, or netball for Japanese women.

- Invite Japanese friends into your home, inviting members of their family, and yours, if possible. Young children, especially boys, may be a little more boisterous than you are used to, so don't expect them to sit quietly! If you want them to come again, have something for them all to enjoy.

- Japanese women are often interested in cultural activities unique to their host culture. Anything related to handmade crafts (e.g., quilt making) is a particular favourite.

Being taught to cook Western food is also appreciated. French and Italian food may be well known in Japan, but much other Western food is relatively unknown.

- Flower arrangement is an art associated with Japanese culture, but they may like to learn how to do it Western style.

- They may have something from their own culture, such as Kimono or tea ceremony, that they would love to show you.

- They often take an interest in flowers and plants. A trip to a local conservatory or botanical garden could prove a popular outing.

- Invite Japanese friends to concerts. Live events are popular.

- Offer to help with English practice, perhaps on a regular basis.

- Church mother and toddler groups are often appreciated by Japanese families.

Gender Roles
Traditionally, Japan has been very rigid in its gender role expectations. Men were expected to be strong, tough, in control, dominant over children and women, and to provide for the family. Women were to be reserved, subservient, to obey their husbands and generally stay at home doing

housework and caring for the children. Though many women go out to work, many of them are likely to remain in relatively subordinate roles. In many businesses there is a real 'glass ceiling' limiting women's promotion prospects. However, women have been expected to manage almost everything in the home, including the childcare and all educational issues.

Snapshot: A Japanese friend in his thirties worked long hours for a Japanese company in the UK. I taught him English on Friday evenings in his home for several months and got to know him quite well. One evening he told me he'd come to realise that he didn't need to stay in the office so late. Everyone else in the office went home at 5pm so he decided to leave work a couple of hours earlier – at about 6 pm. With his extra time, he decided to do three things: (1) take up an indoor sport, (2) go to Anglo-Japanese society meetings, (3) find out about Christianity! I gave him a bilingual New Testament and he started to read it. Next he read three volumes of Old Testament 'manga' (comic-style books). After that he began asking me questions about Christianity and so I offered to do introductory Bible study with him in Japanese after our English class. We soon got started and his wife and mine joined us.

Men's focus has traditionally been on working hard for their company. The company is given a level of loyalty quite rare these days in Europe and the US. It is fairly normal for them to work long hours, coming home at ten or eleven at night. Many fathers will only see their children on weekends. This is still very true for the older generation but has been changing recently. For example, more young women work full-time if they can find suitable childcare for their children and increasingly their husbands are willing to be involved in the child-rearing and housework. However, compared to western companies many Japanese companies are still less flexible and demand long working hours.

There has also been a real issue with a shortage of nurseries in Japan. Consequently, while their children are small, mothers tend to stay at home with them until they can get a nursery place. The number of Japanese fathers who take their full paternity leave is still very small, even though they are entitled to it by law. It is often the case that while they are placed overseas, their working conditions are much more favourable. This can be a great opportunity for them to form friendships and consider Christianity in a way that could have been much harder for them while they were in Japan.

There may be all kinds of things that Japanese women want to learn about you and your country. However, some of them are too shy to begin building a friendship because they may not have confidence in speaking English. Be prepared to take the initiative in some of the ways suggested above. Some Japanese women, especially those who have accompanied their husbands on business here and may not have a job of their own, might spend a lot of time in their home for fear of not being able to communicate well.

Giving and Receiving Gifts

Gifts are important in Japanese culture. If you receive a present, you should express genuine thanks at the time you receive the gift, and then again when you say goodbye. Furthermore, the next time you meet, a comment on the gift of the last visit may be appropriate.

If you are invited to a Japanese person's home, take a gift such as food, drink or flowers, however small, with you. In Japanese society, a gift given is to be met with a gift in return. The Japanese do not always open a gift when they receive it, particularly in a large group of people, so don't be concerned if they don't open yours. If you want to open theirs, this is quite acceptable, but it is best to ask if you may open it.

Enjoying Food Together

The restaurant, rather than the home, is usually where entertaining is done in Japan. So coming into your home for a meal will be a new experience in more ways than one. But this too can be a great opportunity to build deeper friendships. You might want to give some thought to what food you serve. A dish you are familiar with and enjoy yourself is usually best, rather than something that fits your stereotype of Japanese food. Table conversation may also be new to them, especially if wives are invited. Be prepared for it to take a while for them to relax and make conversation.

Make the most of birthdays. Make or buy a cake for them and sing 'Happy Birthday to You' in English – many will already know it. This will probably be a cultural experience for them.

Introductions to Others
Do you know people studying the same subject or in the same line of business as your Japanese friend? Since the Japanese are typically hesitant to introduce themselves to others, and usually rely on go-betweens, an introduction to someone in the same field would be warmly appreciated.

Helping with English
Show sensitivity in your use of the English language and humour. Speak clearly, but not deliberately slowly as this may come across as condescending and offensive.

When your friend doesn't understand and asks you to repeat what you said, do just that. Don't try to rephrase it at first. That may only add to the confusion. Eventually if there is no understanding, write it down. Your friend will have spent six to eight years studying written English and may have a greater reading ability than speaking. They can easily search the meaning by using their phone too.

During conversation, give plenty of verbal and non-verbal affirmatives – frequent nods, saying 'yes' and maintaining occasional eye contact – as you listen to your friend speak. People give much more feedback in Japanese conversations than is typical in the West.

Be careful of using too many idioms and provide explanations when you do use one. For example, if you say that 'it's raining cats and dogs', explain that this means it's raining very heavily. Most Japanese will appreciate learning the meanings of common expressions. They may have struggled through lists of English idioms while at school, so they are fascinated when they hear some in use. You could also ask them about similar idioms in Japanese.

Helping with Everyday Life

In the early weeks of your friend's stay, travel may be a problem. Offer to help with buying bus or train tickets and going into town. You can also tell them about some useful websites for local information and transport apps for their mobile phone.

Shopping is another concern. In Japan, it's common to go shopping each day for that evening's meal. Japanese people who want to do their own cooking will want to know where to shop for groceries. Offer to take them along when you go shopping. Comparing Japanese and Western methods of grocery shopping makes an excellent conversation topic. If you know of Asian supermarkets, they may be grateful for this local information.

Babysitting is not something they will have been used to in Japan, outside the immediate family. A husband's heavy work schedule may preclude a night out anyway. Don't stop when your first offer is turned down, though. In time it might become more possible for them.

Do your friends have children in school? Their school letters may be quite puzzling. Be ready to offer to explain the contents, and what they need to do. Also offer to help with things such as contracts for utilities and broadband and so on. Official forms can be very hard to understand.

In times of crisis, such as an illness, an accident, or difficulties with their living situation, your help will be most appreciated. If you can be there to help deal with 'officials' at the hospital or insurance company, then do!

Room for Misunderstanding

With increasing globalization and Western influence, Japanese attitudes and traditions are changing. The following points are only a rough guide; older Japanese people are more likely to adhere to these traditions and customs than younger ones.

Do's and Don'ts

- If you invite a Japanese friend to visit you any time, be sure to give a specific invitation for a set time and make sure the details are understood, perhaps giving a written note of time and place. Japanese friendships begin in a very structured way.

- When Japanese friends visit, if you put out a plate of biscuits and offer them one, don't be surprised if they don't take one. Being polite in the traditional Japanese way, they are waiting for you to repeat the offer!

- If you go to your friend's home for lunch, expecting a light snack, but get a huge meal and don't leave until four o'clock, next time, make sure you know what you have been invited to – maybe explaining what time you will have to leave. Entertaining guests is important in Japanese culture.

- Don't sit or lean back on a desk or table when you are talking or teaching. Japanese people may struggle with your dishonouring of the place of learning with a baser part of your anatomy! Japanese never sit on any furniture which is not a chair. Sitting with your feet on a table may well cause offence.

- The Western habit of walking in dirty shoes on nice clean carpets can surprise Japanese people. In Japan, it is customary to wear slippers inside. If you visit a Japanese person's house, they may not insist you wear slippers (provided) but do it anyway – they will feel much more at ease. When coming into your house they may wonder if they should take off their shoes. Assure them that it is OK to walk on your carpet in outside shoes – if you're happy with that. Alternatively, if you have Japanese visitors more often, you could have a few pairs of spare slippers ready near the door for their use.

Customs

- Japanese people traditionally bow to one another. This is the normal way of greeting in Japan. Some may be more used to shaking hands than others.

- As already mentioned, giving gifts is common in Japanese society – it's extremely rare to visit someone without taking a gift. However, if someone gives you a very large gift, it might be a way of saying 'thank you very much for all your help, but I'll not be seeing you anymore.'

- When they eat a meal, they may pick up the soup bowl. In Japan, soup bowls do not have a rim, and the bowl is picked up and soup drunk from the bowl as from a cup.

- They might slurp the soup! In many cultures, Japan included, slurping is a sign of enjoyment of the food. Noodles too are slurped with satisfaction. Some may have learnt that this is impolite in the West, but not all remember it.

- It is more polite in Japan to sniff than to blow your nose in public. Japanese people will excuse themselves and go elsewhere if they really need to blow their nose. They use tissues; handkerchiefs are only used to mop the brow.

- Japanese people may smile at what may seem to be inappropriate moments for those in Western cultures. Japanese smiles and laughter are often puzzling to outsiders and may be regarded ambivalently. A smile can be a sign of friendliness, an expression of reserve, an open display of emotions, an indication of embarrassed self-consciousness or an indication of understanding or not understanding. For women, embarrassment often causes smiles or giggles, and sad or even devastating news may bring a set smile that covers confusion or deep emotions.

- You may ask your friend something and get no answer at all. They are probably not ignoring you: in some situations, silence counts as a valid reply. It may be that the question is embarrassing for some reason, or simply that they do not know the answer. Unless you are sure they didn't hear you properly, it's probably best to change the subject.

CHAPTER THREE

Witnessing to Japanese People[1]

In Japan, Christianity has historically been considered the religion of the West. It's possible that to the extent your Japanese friend admires or dislikes the West, they admire or dislike Christianity. If your friend has chosen to visit a country where Christianity is much more deeply rooted in the culture than in Japan, there is a good chance that they may have a positive feeling towards Christianity itself. This is a wonderful opportunity to share our precious faith.

As noted earlier, Christian-style weddings are common in Japan and your friend may have attended one. Also, many Japanese people will have been to, or know about, well-respected

---

1 See also the Appendix: Ten Obstacles to Communicating the Gospel with Japanese People.

Christian kindergartens, schools and universities. On the other hand, there can be barriers to Japanese people thinking that they themselves could become Christians. This is even more the case when they come to understand the demands Jesus places on full allegiance to him, forsaking all other gods.

Other hindrances may be a strong background of 'scientific atheism', or perhaps a suspicion of enthusiastic religion in society or in history.[2]

Talking to Japanese People About Christianity

One of the best ways to share the message of Jesus with your Japanese friend is to read the Bible together with them. (See especially the section on 'Bible Study' below.) Also, inviting them along to your church, a Christian gathering, a course introducing Christianity, or a special event, would be good things to do.

Of course, it is always good to ask questions about what our friends believe, or what they think about spiritual matters. Bear in mind that the word 'God' (*kami*) in Japanese usually has a very different meaning from 'Eternal Creator' – so it is best not to assume that you mean the same thing by that word. Talking about praying for things is also not unusual for most Japanese people, and along with this you can share about how your faith and practice of being a disciple

---

2 See also the Appendix: Ten Issues to Cover when Discipling.

of Jesus impacts the way you live. If you can share how you understood and begun to follow the God of the Bible, that too could open up new understanding for your friend.

Talk About Intelligent Design

The Japanese have a great love of nature. We can easily explain that we believe the world we live in, with all its beauty, did not come about by chance. Japanese schools teach evolutionary theory, and Japanese people often place a high view on academia and are very reluctant to challenge what they've been taught. For some Japanese people, the opening words of Genesis can have a powerful effect, showing that the universe was deliberately created.

Ask What They Think About God

Rather than asking if they believe in God, ask them what they think about him, as this is less threatening. Japanese people sometimes take the view that a person only 'enters a religion' if they have a problem they cannot cope with. To avoid being thought of as not coping, such people may prefer not to say if they believe in God.

Some Japanese people overseas may be under pressure from their families to steer clear of Christianity. This is especially likely with first-born sons, who have the main responsibility to continue the worship of ancestors. There may be times when your friend does not want to talk about spiritual matters anymore or becomes wary of Christians. Be patient and try to respect their spiritual 'comfort zone'. Be a genuine friend and pray for God to provide the right opportunities for you to talk.

Japanese friends may appear to accept what you say because you are the teacher and because they want to please you. They may also say 'yes, I understand', or answer 'yes' when you ask them if they agree – which may be more out of a desire to be polite, than to indicate actual assent. So don't be too quick to assume they are ready to make a commitment to Christ at an early stage. There is a danger in pushing them too far, too fast. They may respond and wish they had not, and then the only way they know of backtracking could be to drop out altogether.

Bible Study

As a simple way into this topic, you could ask if they have read much of the Bible, and if so, what they thought about it. You could then explain that you enjoy reading the Bible and ask if they would like to do a basic study of some passages together with you. As you can see from the examples in the box below, it can be better to do this with a group or one-to-one. Ask the Holy Spirit to give you guidance, as well as warmth and courage as you ask.

If your friend/friends are willing to study the Bible together with you, then try to get a bilingual

Bible or New Testament (preferably with modern Japanese) for them, or an English one in a modern translation.[3] Using a pre-prepared study specifically written for Japanese people means that the person writing the study will have considered the Japanese cultural and intellectual context in preparing questions. In addition, if it is bilingual, your friend will be able to check understanding of the question being considered, even if (as is often the case) they are keen to stick mostly to English.

Group or 1-to-1?

Example A: 'When my English friend offered to look at the Bible together with me, I was interested, but I was worried what my other Japanese friends would think, so I said no'. Then later, when asked again in a private conversation, I was very happy to say yes'.

Example B: 'I don't think I would have wanted to do a Bible study one-on-one with my Australian Christian friend – I would have been uncomfortable and worried about getting things wrong. But when she asked me and two other friends, we thought it would be fun and interesting to do together, so we said yes, and had a great time meeting together'.

---

3 Some good bilingual resources for Bible study, including Bibles, can be found in the Further Resources section at the end of the book.

If you are not using a study guide, perhaps for a short introduction, you could look at Genesis 1:1-3, or John 3:16. One idea for study would be to invite your friend to look together at a Psalm or another passage that has meant a lot to you personally. Luke 15 is also a great passage for explaining the kind of God you believe in, and you can also use it to share about your own story of 'coming home' to God.

For a series of studies, you could start by looking at Genesis 1-3, to introduce the God of the Bible (remember that Japanese people will usually have quite a different concept of God), human beings, the fall – and more! Going through a Gospel, perhaps Mark or Luke, or selecting a few passages which you're familiar with from some of the Gospels could also be a good idea.

In terms of how to conduct the study, it may be useful to have questions written down, and to focus mainly on questions for which the answers are in the Bible passage. If they have thought about the question for a short while, but don't seem to be able to find a good answer, suggestions, hints, or letting them know the answer can be the best way forward. It can be a good idea to encourage writing down their answers.

As with any Bible study, as you prepare, ask for the Holy Spirit to help in creating a good atmosphere, to help you know how to explain things, and to give understanding to your friend. Also, for discernment about whether, and how, to follow up on diversions that occur, and on how long to let the study go on for. Offering to pray for your friend at the end of the study could be a good idea if it feels comfortable to do so, but it's probably best not to ask your friend to pray themselves, unless they'd like to.

Responding to Shinto and Buddhism:
Few people in Japan know the traditional Buddhist and Shinto teachings, and Japanese people visiting the West are unlikely to defend these religions except to protect themselves from Christianity. However, if your friend is interested in these religions, listen carefully to the way they describe it. Always try to understand before offering any answer or alternative to their beliefs. Resist the urge to dispute a point before understanding it (Proverbs 18:13).

Questions Japanese People Ask
Japanese people will face a range of issues as they think about becoming Christians. Westerners who do not know their language may find it a challenge to help with them all. It is better to wait until your friend raises any questions with you rather than bringing them up yourself. The following questions are some of the most frequently asked:

Q. Can I believe in Jesus and still follow other religions?

Since most Japanese people take part in rites of more than one religion, your friend may be surprised to hear that the answer to this question is 'no'. It is therefore important to explain *why* this is the case. Becoming a Christian is not about becoming a consumer of a particular service – in the same way that you could have a coffee loyalty card, a golf club membership, and an annual zoo pass without any problem. You can use the Bible to show that becoming a believer in Jesus is to belong to and come into close relationship with the God of the Bible – and in the same way that you cannot belong to more than one marriage (or more than one sports team, or company) at one time, that it is an exclusive relationship.

However, this doesn't mean that Japanese Christians cannot attend family Buddhist ceremonies, if they are careful about how they participate. If possible, refer your friend to a Japanese Christian worker to discuss this more fully. Or use some of the contact details at the back of the book for helpful advice, including useful books.

Q. Will my social and family relationships change?

It is good to be honest, and positive, in answering this question. You can stress that the Bible teaches us to be the best son/daughter/husband/wife/friend that we can be. On the other hand, there may be choices we need to make as a Christian that close family or friends will disapprove of. A Christian should be sensitive to others, but not fear what they will think of us. It can be helpful to share stories of real Christians to help illustrate and reassure. There is sometimes misunderstanding in a family when a person becomes a Christian, but in fact the family will gain from the increased love and consideration which now, *by the Holy Spirit*, begins to flow from the new believer's heart.

Encouraging openness is important. It is advisable for a wife to seek her husband's agreement if she wants to be baptized. When she trusts in Christ, encourage her to pray for her husband's salvation (1 Pet. 3:1-6). Inviting them over for a meal as a couple may help defuse any suspicions the husband may have.

Whether children tell their parents in Japan of their interest in Christianity must be left up to them, but if that interest leads to baptism, they should be strongly encouraged to do so.

If you can develop a relationship with parents, by sending Christmas cards or a photo of yourself with your friend, this will head off some difficulties and help reduce suspicion. If the parents come over to visit, look after them well and let them get to know you, so they see you are not a member of a cult trying to 'kidnap' their offspring, but that you are a genuine friend to the whole family.

Q. What about relationships at work?

Japanese people usually spend long hours on the job, although often conditions away from Japan (especially in Europe) will be less demanding than they might have been used to back home. Socializing together after work is traditionally considered very important; this is all part of building team spirit in the office or factory. Many jobs in Japan, and in Japanese companies in the West, adversely affect a Christian's home life. Try to get a feel for the kind of pressures Japanese families face in this way.

Some Japanese men will recognize that their commitment to Christ would affect how they conduct business and may hinder advancement. Share Jesus' claim that those who give up anything for him in this life will be reimbursed now, and in the age to come (Mark 10:29-31). Introduce new Japanese Christians to other Christians with similar professional interests. If there are none in your church, you could contact others through one of the Japanese Christian Fellowships or interdenominational organisations (see the details at the back of the book). Pray that God would help them see ways of living as a Christian in their workplace.

Help businessmen to think through the issues of how they will be able to maintain good relationships with colleagues at work, and at the same time recognize their family responsibilities and the value of developing wholesome, Christian friendships.

Others may wonder if they will lose their jobs

or rapport with colleagues if they take a stand for Christ. Show your friend the accounts in Daniel (1:8-16; 3:1-30; 6:1-28) that demonstrate how God honours his reputation and works on behalf of those who take a stand for him. Work through Scriptures that will enable your friend to take the most appropriate stand when necessary. Try to be sympathetic and understanding about pressures that you will probably never have to face.

Q. Will I lose my identity as a Japanese person if I trust Jesus?
Certain traditions in Japan, including many of the regular seasonal events, are strongly influenced by Buddhist or Shinto world views. So, some Japanese will feel that their national identity will be lost if they follow Christ and stop following these traditions.

It's important to explain that Christianity is not a Western religion. It began in the Middle East – and should be called an Asian religion! You can emphasize that the Bible was written out of Middle Eastern cultures that have much more in common with Asia than with the West. Help your Japanese friend to see that not all Westerners are Christian. It may be helpful to explain that there is a difference between nominal or 'cultural' Christians, and those who have a real heart experience of Christ.

You could also find out about and speak of the fairly well-known Japanese people who have been fine Christians, such as Inazo Niitobe (political activist and author), Kanzo Uchimura (author, evangelist, and founder of the Non-Church Christian Movement), Toyohiko Kagawa (campaigner for social justice) and Ayako Miura (best-selling author). All of these have books in English as well as in Japanese. Point out that a person is not giving up being Japanese, but only giving up Buddhism or Shinto and that the Bible says we find our identity in Christ. Meeting Christians from other cultures will help illustrate that God is the God of the whole world. You could show your friend Christ's command to take the gospel to every nation (Matt. 28:19).

Your friend may not realize before they return to Japan all the changes they will need to make as they follow Jesus there. So when they do return, it is important to connect them with a Christian in Japan who can follow up with them and help them work through these issues. If possible, a three-way video call to introduce them, would be a great way to do that.[4]

Q. What about New Year traditions?

Every New Year is preceded by parties towards the end of December, called *bo-nen-kai* ('forget-the-year') parties, when people often drink heavily. Almost certainly a Christian will have

---

4 See the Further Resources and Contacts sections at the back of the book for resources to help Japanese Christians as they return to Japan.

to attend functions in the office and will need to work out the appropriate way to behave. Show how it is possible to celebrate New Year and other holidays in a Christian way. One church in Japan plans 'remember-the-year' parties: a Christian alternative to the excessive drinking common at *bo-nen-kai* parties. People share in public how God has helped them over the past year. They give thanks, and the tone of the party is one of celebration.

On New Year's Day and other times around the holiday, non-Christian families visit Shinto shrines and pray for the blessing of the gods for the coming year. Again, many churches hold New Year's Day services, and you can encourage your friend to attend them if possible. Show your friend how we depend on God and pray to him for guidance and blessing when beginning a new year, or any new experience.

Q. My family will expect me to worship at the god-shelf.

Ancestor worship, or ancestor veneration, is often regarded as a duty in family life (see chapter 2). Help your friend see that one can be a very loyal son or daughter without worshipping at the family god-shelf or the Buddhist home altar. Explain that it is good to remember a deceased relative and thank God for the good things that came to them, and through them, without involving the worship of, or connection to, that person's spirit.

In some families, it is a regular habit to pray and make offerings at the family god-shelf. In other families, offerings are only made at times of crisis as it is traditionally believed spirits can cause these crises. Encourage your friend to talk with relatives about the Christian faith long before any crisis where they may be called upon to offer incense to the spirit of the deceased. Sharing good memories of the deceased person will always help the family, as will openness about how the Christian prays for other family members.

If your friend wishes to explain his family's approach to the spirits of the deceased, be a sensitive and willing listener. At some point you may want to read a passage together – like 1 John 4:1-4 which differentiates among spirits. Or you may point out texts such as 2 Corinthians 2:14 and Colossians 1:15-20, which highlight the supremacy of Christ over the spiritual world.

Q. What about all the different denominations?

The question of denominations is likely to arise if your friend has an awareness of different parts of the Christian church. It is best to say that there is a difference between cults such as Jehovah's Witnesses and Mormons (both very active in Japan), and mainline churches. You can explain that Catholics, Protestants and Orthodox churches all believe the foundational truths of the Nicene creed, but that there are still differences in what they believe.

Avoid complicated explanations about differences between Christian denominations. It is worth saying that just as there are historical reasons for the many different branches of Buddhism, so there are different branches of Christianity, but there are core beliefs, consistent with the Bible, which all the major churches have agreed on for the majority of Christian history.

Aspects of Christianity Which Appeal to Japanese People

In western culture, the appeal to trust in Christ may be made in a variety of ways. We may appeal to truth, to fulfilment in this life, to the need for forgiveness, or to life with God in heaven. For a Japanese person, this may be difficult to understand. The following appeals are often particularly effective with Japanese people:

God Has the First Claim on Our Loyalty.
For someone from a non-Christian family, the idea of separation from unbelieving family members can make the decision to trust Christ difficult. Remind your friend that the Bible presents God as the creator of the whole universe. Human beings are created by God, to joyfully know and serve him – this is how we truly fulfil our purpose. Family and social relationships take second place in the light of this eternal relationship. It may be helpful to see how, in Jesus' parable, the rich man who was separated from God was anxious that his family would 'not also come to this place of torment' (Luke 16:28).

If this view of God seems strange to your friend, be patient. Keep pointing to texts in the Bible that show God to be the God of the whole world (e.g. Acts 17:24-31).

The Family of God

The question of identity within a group is often of more concern for Japanese than the question of ultimate truth, so cultivate a relationship that includes plenty of group activities with other Christians. If your friend is a student, you could introduce them to the Christian Union or a Bible study for international students.

As you engage in group activities, be sensitive to how Japanese friends feel around you and other Christian friends. Do you accept them as members of your group, or are you still looking on them as outsiders? How are others treated in your group? Even if you fully accept your Japanese friends, they may be offended if someone else is not treated well by group members.

If at all possible, take your friend to a Japanese church or fellowship group in your area. It is important that those who become Christians in the West meet other Japanese who worship Christ. This will give them a feel for what it might be like to be a Christian in Japan.[5]

When your friend experiences misunderstanding from others or expresses concern

5 See the back of the book for details of Japanese fellowships, including organisations focused on helping Japanese Christians returning home.

about pressures from the family back in Japan, you could refer to texts such as Mark 3:31-35 or Luke 8:19-21. These describe Jesus' true family. If your own relationships within the family of God are a source of personal strength, your friend will be motivated to follow Christ and to be part of God's family. Always be willing to listen and to pray things through.

Going to Church

It is good to consider when is the best time to introduce a Japanese person to a church service, whether in Japanese or English. Choose a special event like Christmas or Easter, or a church concert, to introduce them to church. Your Japanese friends often want to experience a church service in the local language as part of learning culture, and as a way to meet local people. So don't be shy of bringing them to your own small groups or home groups, if the atmosphere is open and welcoming. If there is a Japanese church within travelling distance, it is also good to visit there before your friend returns to Japan to experience something of what church life back in Japan will be like.

Sin and Shame

It is good to consider differences in cultural backgrounds by thinking about the different roles that 'shame' and 'honour' play. In traditional Japanese culture, there is much more awareness of what others will think of you, especially if an action or a person will make them disapprove of you. In terms of standards of behaviour taught from a young age, 'causing a nuisance' or 'being an embarrassment' is spoken of as something to be desperately avoided, in a similar way that being 'the guilty party' or 'being in the wrong' is seen as something to avoid in other cultures. This means instead of words such as 'sin', words such as 'humiliation' or 'disgrace' better describe the depth of feeling behind this consequence of regrettable actions. Terms such as 'crime' or 'guilt' are taken as more technical legal terms (though potentially bringing with them great shame too).[6]

When you discuss the concept of sin with your friend be sure to show the shame that sin causes. You can show from Genesis 2:25–3:21 how shame came upon humanity with sin. Genesis 2:25 and 3:5-11 are especially important verses. If your friend wishes to talk, be ready to listen to how he or she understands moral evil and also the social force we know as shame. You could describe how God, in Christ, has delivered and is delivering you from sin and the shame it brings in your own life. And if even after becoming a Christian, your friend comments on being ashamed of something, explain how Christ has solved sin's shame problem, by bearing our shame for us, and taking it with him to the cross and grave.

---

6 honorshame.com is a useful resource to explore this concept.

When Your Friend Becomes a Christian

God alone brings Christian growth (Phil. 1:6), but there are a few practical ways you can help your Japanese friends to grow and be established in their new-found faith.

Find a Social Network

Once a commitment to Christ has been made, it is crucial that your friend becomes part of a network of Christians in your area. At the same time, begin praying for integration into Christian fellowship back in Japan.

If the new Christian is married, pray for and encourage them to speak openly with their spouse about their new faith. Pray also for unmarried Japanese people as unbelieving families can put pressure on single Japanese Christians to marry non-Christians. Women may have noticed that they outnumber men in most churches and so be anxious about their prospects of finding a Christian husband. Explain how you are praying and offer encouragement to ask God for his guidance in these areas. Marriage is the norm in Asia but there are signs of change in this area and in Japan the age at which people get married is steadily rising.

Find out where in Japan your friend will be living. Talk to somebody who knows the country. If you don't know anyone with connections in Japan, connect with one of the agencies listed at the back of this book. Your friend is much more likely to join a church back home if you can provide an introduction.

Find a Place to Serve

One key to Japanese effectiveness at work is that people act as a team. This is taught from primary school days and is true in most clubs and societies in Japan. The same is true in vibrant Japanese churches. Each member is given a particular role.

Following on from your friend's commitment to Christ, they need to take steps to become truly part of the life of a local church. Think about what this could be. In terms of serving, bear in mind that your friend may find it difficult to say no to a commitment, so sensitivity is required. When encouraging them to serve, be mindful of your friend's business responsibilities or academic workload but encourage them to give concrete expression to their new-found faith (1 Cor. 12:12-31).

Allow for Japanese Expression of Faith

As you draw Japanese friends into the life and community of a church, be aware that people throughout the world worship God differently. In the West we tend to focus on surface appearances – a soloist who you think did an admirable job at church may appear to be a 'show-off' to Japanese.

After a Sunday service at your church, ask your Japanese friends what they liked or disliked about the service. Resist the temptation to defend the style of worship in your church. Listen in order to understand how your friend approaches Christian worship.

Of course, you will want to help your friend grow in their relationship with God by good habits of listening to Jesus in the Bible and praying to the Father. Pray that God would reveal to your friend what it means to be 'in Christ' (Eph. 1:3-14). Also pray together that God would guide both of you in your Christian lives (Phil. 1:3-6). Pray that you would both grow in confidence as Christians and in your personal prayer lives and become regular in Bible reading.

Baptism

Baptism may feel like a very big step for a Japanese person, for a number of reasons. Try to get them to speak to a Japanese pastor or another Japanese Christian (or someone who has worked with the church in Japan) even if only by phone, before taking this step. It's best if spouses talk things over, and younger people should be encouraged to consider how their families would feel about such a step. Those getting baptized in a western church will miss out on the extensive baptismal preparation they would receive in a Japanese-speaking church. However, there may be reasons for getting baptized before returning to Japan. The question of where to get baptized needs prayerful consideration.

Back Home in Japan

It may be that your friend returns to Japan having decided to live as a Christian. Or perhaps your friend has not made a decision but wants to continue to engage with Christianity after going back to Japan. Perhaps they are considering getting baptized after they return to Japan, or they may have taken that step already.

It is worth spending considerable effort to introduce the returning Christian, or seeker, to the church in Japan. If they are able to navigate reverse culture shock fruitfully, and persevere in following Jesus, they can be a wonderful resource for renewal and evangelism in their own surroundings, whether this is a new area for them, or in the same place they lived before travelling overseas. Their experience of Christian community overseas means that they can bring good new ideas into the fellowship or motivate brothers and sisters in Christ to take on challenges which they had been tempted to give up on. All this takes care, sensitivity and time. A great deal depends on getting the 're-entry' right.

Help your friend to make use of the resources that are available to specifically help with this transition. If possible, look together with them at a study guide designed to help Japanese people returning to their home country. There are also conferences and groups set up specifically to help people in this situation.[7]

---

7 See the Further Resources and Contacts sections for these in your location

Returning to Japan and settling into a Japanese church, having experienced Christianity in the West, is very often difficult. There are several reasons for this.

First, with Sunday being the only free day for social, sports and family activities, there is a lot more competition for the use of Sunday mornings than they likely experienced when they were overseas. Second, the church culture may seem very strange compared to what they experienced overseas. Not only will there be cultural differences, but for some, something they readily accepted at a 'foreign' church overseas, may seem much stranger to them when it is in their own language and in their own country.

Snapshot: 'It feels really weird to me to hear and say the Japanese word for "Jesus". I was really comfortable talking and hearing about "Jesus" in English, but it has a completely different feeling when I hear it in Japanese.'

Japanese seeker,
on returning to Japan and attending church there
a few times

At their local church in Japan, there is likely to be only a small group of people; the average congregation is 30 people. New Christians may be wary about joining such a small group – sometimes mainly children and housewives – because they may feel that a large burden will fall on their shoulders, both in finance, to support the pastor, and in time, to serve on committees. They may also feel that they do not fit in, in terms of their demographic, or life experience, or personality.

It may well be the case that the pastor of the church they join in Japan is stricter about involvement in all aspects of church life, and this can seem to put extra pressures on your friend to conform. Some people feel embarrassed because work or study commitments mean that they cannot attend prayer meetings, so they stop attending all church gatherings altogether.

Japanese churches are increasingly aware of some of these problems, and are working to make it easier for those who return from overseas to fit in. They may have an English worship service run by a foreigner that could be a bridge back into the Japanese church. For some, it is easier to fit into a church run by a foreign missionary, and in some areas, there are 'returnee' groups which exist to ease the transition. However, in the end, we want to help our friends to fit into the normal Japanese church, contribute to the worship and witness of that local fellowship of believers, and to be an effective Christian witness in the society they go back to.

The best way to help your friend make a good connection with a local community of believers in Japan, is to find a personal link to a Christian who lives near to where your friend is returning. This might be done through a church or organisation you trust. If possible, a video call with the three of you to introduce one another and begin a relationship with someone who will follow up with your friend, will go a long way to help this happen.

Further Resources

Suggested Reading
(not all authors listed here are Christian)

<u>Prayer Guide</u>
Beneath the Surface: 30 Ways to Pray for Japan, OMF, Pioneers 2020.

<u>Missionary Biographies / Testimonies</u>
In Japan the crickets cry, Ronald Clements & Steve Metcalf, 2010.

On Giants' Shoulders, Patrick McElligott, 4th revised ed., 2013.

Konnichi wa Kiwi! Warren Payne, 2008.

Jesus did many other things as well. Short stories out of Japan, Tony Schmidt, 2017.

Ultimate Grace, Levi Booth, 2019.

Treasures gained in this land, Ruth Dueck, 2021.

Utterly Amazed, Miriam Davis, 2021.

<u>By Japanese Christian authors</u>
Buddhist Priest Meets Jesus, Hirokazu Matsuoka, 2013.

Shiokari Pass, Ayako Miura, 1968.

Cultural Differences:
One World, Two Minds, Denis Lane, OMF, 1995 (Kindle).

Japanese Society/Culture
An Introduction to Japanese Society, 4th ed; Sugimoto Yoshio, CUP 2014.

Japan Through the Looking Glass, Alan MacFarlane, Profile Books 2017.

Polite Fictions: Why Japanese and Americans Seem Rude to Each Other, Nancy Sakamoto & Reiko Naotsuka, 1982.

Shutting Out the Sun: How Japan Created Its Own Lost Generation, Michael Zielenziger, Doubleday 2006.

The Unseen Face of Japan, 2nd ed; David Lewis, Wide Margin, 2013.

The Japanese Mind, Roger J Davies & O Ikeno, Tuttle, 2002.

Japanese History

A Brief History of Japan, Jonathan Clements, Tuttle, *2017*

Modern Japan – A Very Short Introduction, Christopher Goto-Jones, OUP 2009.

General Resources

<u>Japan Resources for Missions</u>
sites.google.com/view/
japanresourcesformissions/home

<u>Online Newspapers:</u>
The Japan Times, The Asahi Shimbun,
The Mainichi, BBC News Japan.

Japanese / Bilingual Bibles

Japanese Bibles and New Testaments are available in the UK from the Japan Christian Link bookshop <u>jclglobal.org/bookshop</u> and in the US from the Japanese Christian Bookstore <u>japanesechristianbookstore.com.</u>

For Bible study, we recommend the Shinkaiyaku version which is used widely in evangelical churches in Japan. The Japanese Living Bible translation is good for those who want to read the Bible for themselves as it's easier to understand.

YouVersion has the Japanese Living Bible translation available for free download <u>bible.com/</u> <u>app</u> onto phones, tablets and computers.

JLB – Japanese Living Bible, biblegateway.com.

Bible Study Resources:

Bilingual Bible Study by former OMF missionary to Japan: lifechangingtruthjp.com.

Bilingual Bible study texts available to order from the UK: jclglobal.org.

'Curious' by Katsuya Iida, J-Publications, available on Amazon.com.

Christianity Explored Japanese Edition: the-goodbook.co.uk/translations/japanese/.

The Alpha Course (available in Japanese and English) alpha.org.

The Bible project in Japanese: bibleproject.com/japanese/.

Mustard Seed online bilingual introductory and discipleship Bible studies: mustardseedosaka.com/resources-overview.

Useful Contacts

OMF International Japanese Returnee Focus Team is a global team of OMF workers who specialize in helping Japanese people to find faith in Christ, grow as disciples, and return to Japan as lifelong fruitful Christians. They would be delighted to help with any stage of this process and can be contacted via:

returnee.japanese@omfmail.com

OMF.org

Telephone numbers:
OMF International US: 800.422.5330
OMF International UK: 01732 887299
OMF International Australia: (02) 9868 4777

Reaching Japanese for Christ Network

rjcnetwork.org

Links to many further resources. North America based, but much of the information provided is relevant to people in other parts of the world.

Japanese Christian Fellowship Network (JCFN)

jcfn.org (English/Japanese bilingual)

JCFN has the specific aim of helping those who have become Christians overseas to find fellowship and support as they return to Japan. They are based in California and Tokyo, but will help people from anywhere in the world.

Japan Christian Link (JCL)

jclglobal.org

JCL are the best place in the UK to get hold of Japanese Bibles, Christian books, tracts and other resources and also have a list of Japanese churches, fellowships and meetings in the UK.

Japan Connect Australia

japanconnect.au

Networking site for Oceania (including list of Japanese churches).

Contacts in Other Places:

There is Japanese ministry going on in many other places. If you try enquiring with one or more of the organisations mentioned above they can almost certainly use their own networks to give you a useful contact.

Appendixes

Top Ten ...

... Ways to Build Relationships

... Ideas for Helping Japanese People Practically

... Key Aspects of Japanese Culture

... Obstacles to Communicating the Gospel

... Ways to Get Involved Where You Are Now

... Issues to Cover When Discipling

... Challenges of Returning to a Japanese Church

Ten Ways to Build Relationships

1. **GOING TO A CAFE** or eating out together is an easy way to start building a relationship. It's normally best to share the bill, as this will help them feel relaxed and not be in debt to you.

2. **POLITENESS** is equated with being restrained and unassertive. If you offer something you will probably need to ask them twice before it's accepted.

3. **GIFT**-giving is an important part of Japanese culture, especially when visiting someone's home for the first time. Appreciation is often expressed by giving gifts.

4. **ASK** about their family, birth month or hometown. Look for common connections such as the same age, favourite foods or places you have visited.

5. **ENJOY** doing things together. Find out their hobbies. Offer to go for a walk or a short trip to a place of interest. Arrange to play some sport together, or go to see a concert/football match etc.

6. **BE COMPLIMENTARY** as they speak English with you. Gently correcting big mistakes will be appreciated. Affirm how well they are doing as they relate their various experiences of living in a different culture.

7. **INVITE** them to your home; introduce them to your family. Ask to see their family photos. Show a few of yours.

8. **CELEBRATE** dates that are special to them like New Year. Ask them to celebrate Christmas or Easter with you. Explain the meaning of them briefly.

9. **ASK THEM TO HELP** you learn something Japanese: origami, calligraphy, cooking, or simple words and phrases. Organize a Japanese evening and ask them to take part.

10. **PRACTICAL HELP** is indispensable in building trust. For ideas in helping them in various ways see the next section.

Ten Ideas for Helping Japanese People Practically

1. **OFFER** to help them fill in forms, e.g: bank accounts, and register with a doctor or dentist. Help them choose between the many deals for internet providers, mobile phones or other services.

2. **OFFER** to teach them some English (you don't have to be a qualified English teacher!). If it's regular, they may feel more comfortable paying you. Tell them of any nearby, free English classes.

3. **TEACH** them how to cook local food. Advise them on where to shop, e.g. where to find fresh fish. Offer to take them shopping when they first arrive.

4. **HELP** them to find parent and toddlers groups and buy school supplies. Advise them what to ask for in the hairdressers.

5. **SUGGEST** you teach them something of local life and culture. Invite them to ask questions.

6. **CHECK** they know how to buy bus or train tickets. Tell them about cheaper tickets, discount bus/rail cards etc.

7. **HELP** them plan a journey – if they are planning to travel. Tell them about places worth visiting.

8. **OFFER** to give them an hour or two to help with whatever they need. Ask when is a good time to come.

9. **INVITE** them to your church and make them feel welcome. Tell them that anyone, not only Christians, can attend. Explain in simple, non-religious words, what happens in the service and around the church. Introduce them to one or two of your church friends.

10. **FOLLOW UP** – With all these offers Japanese people may decline or hesitate to accept at first, as they won't want to bother you. If you do offer to do something for them, be sure to follow up and actually do it.

Ten Key Aspects of Japanese Culture

1. **RELATIONSHIPS** are central to Japanese cultural attitudes. They take longer to establish, but good ones last forever.

2. **HARMONY** between people is highly valued. Japanese are polite, kindly spoken and careful in expressing strong opinions. Blame is not placed on others publicly to maintain this harmony.

3. **TRUST** is foundational. It is established slowly through mutual acknowledgement of the sincerity and consistency of words and actions.

4. **TRADITION** carries great authority. Japanese tend to conform to the way things have always been done.

5. **HIERARCHY** means that respect is always shown to those in positions above oneself. Japanese will defer decision making to those with more expertise, greater experience or who are older.

6. **MODESTY** requires Japanese speak deprecatingly of themselves and their family, and favourably of others.

7. **PUBLIC FACE** is given priority over personal opinion. Nothing is said that might cause others shame or embarrassment. Blatant refusal, 'no' is avoided. 'Yes' doesn't necessarily imply full agreement.

8. **RELIGION** is expressed through Buddhist ritual and Shinto ceremony, not personal devotion. Funerals in particular are considered very important. Most people do not see themselves as 'religious'.

9. **OVERSEAS** Japanese will normally try to adapt to local cultural attitudes including Christian ones. So don't worry too much about trying to adapt perfectly to Japanese culture.

10. **ON RETURN** to Japan cultural values acquired overseas will clash with Japanese culture. Readjustment is often a difficult and lonely period when returnees need support.

Ten Obstacles to Communicating the Gospel

1. **THE BIBLE** is little-known, even less read. Explain its authors, languages (not English), historical setting and Jesus-centred message. Bilingual Bibles are available.

2. **GODS** are common but vague. Emphasize the personal creator, the Almighty and all-knowing God. The Trinity can be introduced later.

3. **ATHEISTIC** evolution is widely accepted. Teaching that we are created by God in his image to relate to him is crucial. Detailed discussion of the means of creation is best avoided.

4. **SIN** carries the connotation of criminal activity rather than a self-centred attitude. Shame is felt over poor behaviour but not guilt over failing God.

5. **LOVE** refers to sexual and romantic love but not an act of sacrifice for another. Explain Jesus' death as perfectly expressing such sacrificial love.

6. **FORGIVENESS** may be misunderstood as forbearance, grace as an act of Nature. Japanese are deeply touched by both when experienced through Christ.

7. **REPENTANCE** is confused with mere apology. Emphasize a life-changing decision to turn away from self and follow God.

8. **RELIGION** is seen as primarily ritualistic, faith as a moral virtue. We must model faith as trust in an almighty and wholly dependable God.

9. **SPIRITS** of the ancestors are to be revered. Carefully explain how the Holy Spirit lives within when we believe and is our Comforter and trustworthy Guide.

10. **SALVATION** is commonly thought of as rescue from danger or ill health. Initially explain Jesus' death in terms of reconciliation to a Heavenly Father rather than justification before God.

Ten Ways to Get Involved Where You are Now

1. **Pray** that the LORD gives you one Japanese friend.

2. **Join** a group praying for overseas Japanese – or talk to your pastor and start a group in your church yourself.

3. **Greet** Japanese people, be welcoming and show hospitality. Simplify or slow down your English if necessary.

4. **Start** learning a few basic Japanese phrases.

5. **Read** books about Japan and the Japanese.

6. **Get** in touch with a mission that works amongst the Japanese.

7. **Suggest** a language exchange with a Japanese person. You could teach or talk in English first, then they could teach you Japanese.

8. **Get** some suitable bilingual or Japanese tracts/manga/scripture portions, CD's to pass on to Japanese contacts. Perhaps pass them on to those in your church who have Japanese colleagues.

9. **Offer** – if you have a spare room offer a home stay to a Japanese person in your area. It could be a few days, or longer if that suits.

10. **Contact** – if you have ongoing contact and ministry to Japanese, contact the OMF Diaspora Returnee Ministry team and ask about becoming a co-worker.

Ten Issues to Cover When Discipling[1]

1. **Who am I? My identity in Christ.** It is important to root the disciple's identity in relationship with God. For many Japanese the tendency will be to find identity in their relationship with the disciple-maker.

2. **Forgiveness. I am forgiven and forgiving.** Since human relationships are most important to Japanese people, this area is crucial for personal growth and dynamic Christian witness. Forbearance is a common attitude, forgiveness much rarer.

3. **Guidance. How do I make decisions?** Japanese follow decisions made by those above them. They are likely to defer to your opinion. Teach them how to discern God's voice and follow him.

4. **Family Life. How should I relate to my parents?** Most Japanese who have become Christians abroad return to Japan apprehensive of how their parents will react. Discuss what the Bible means by 'honour your parents'.

5. **Relationships. Questions about marriage and singleness.** Cultural expectations are different from the West though marriage breakdown is increasingly common.

---

1 These 10 areas are covered in The ID Course: International Discipleship available from Friends International (UK).

Introduce biblical principles and allow open discussion on facing marriage and singleness.

6. **Church. I belong to a new community.** Compare the biblical view of church with the disciple's experience abroad. Prepare them to transfer to a Japanese church community that may well have different dynamics.

7. **Culture and Religion. Religious customs concerning death and the afterlife.** Examine the biblical view of honour and respect for the dead. Discuss religious practices in Japan that venerate the dead. For more help contact Japanese Christians and/or OMF Returnee Focus.

8. **How I use my time. Understanding biblical principles of work and rest.** A key area of reverse culture shock and one of trepidation for many returning Japanese. A biblical perspective can greatly ease the transition.

9. **Money and Possessions. How should I use my money?** Materialism is a great temptation in Japan. Encourage returning Japanese people that God is the great Provider. Gently challenge them to contribute generously to his kingdom in Japan.

10. **You shall be my witnesses. How can I tell others about Jesus?** Discuss the many ways we can share our faith in Christ. Excite returnees with the opportunities for witness both in Japan and across the world.

Ten Challenges of Returning to a Japanese Church

1. For a returnee discipled largely in English, it is difficult to read the Bible, pray and understand Christian jargon in Japanese.

2. Returnees find it takes longer to form trusting friendships in Japan. People are more reserved and returnees feel them less warm and welcoming.

3. Returnees struggle to readjust to a formal, hierarchical society; in church, pastors, shown great respect, would never be addressed by their first name for example.

4. Re-entry to a group-oriented society again is a shock. Relearning how to 'read between the lines' and say things that do not disrupt group harmony requires attention and patience.

5. Returnees baptized abroad are sometimes discouraged when told, often justly, by Japanese pastors that their baptismal preparation was quite insufficient to equip them to live as a Christian in a secular world, permeated by Buddhist and Shinto ritual.

6. Some churches distinguish markedly between church members and non-members. Returnees are initially considered the latter and can soon feel isolated and marginalized at church.

7. Japanese churches where few have lived abroad, returnees often feel rejected when the richness of their recent experience is not recognised and they are required to conform to the same pattern as everyone else.

8. Those discipled in Japanese churches overseas enjoy a broader understanding of church. In Japan, showing loyalty both to church and denomination can make them wonder where their loyalty to God lies.

9. Returnees well involved in a Japanese church overseas are frequently frustrated with the slow process of being re-accepted as able to lead ministry in a local Japanese church.

10. Reverse culture shock is exacerbated by the scarcity of Christians in Japan (1 percent officially, 0.3 percent evangelical). It is highly beneficial for a returnee to be linked up with a returnee Christian near where they will live back in Japan.

* * *

The Editors trust this guide to understanding the Japanese people will enable you to be a more effective witness of Jesus Christ. Even though there may be many differences remember that showing love by becoming a friend covers the many lacks we all have. May the Lord make you an even more fruitful Christian.

Christian Focus Publications

Our mission statement
Staying Faithful

In dependence upon God we seek to impact the world through literature faithful to His infallible Word, the Bible. Our aim is to ensure that the Lord Jesus Christ is presented as the only hope to obtain forgiveness of sin, live a useful life and look forward to heaven with Him.

Our Books are published in four imprints:

◁◯✕ CHRISTIAN FOCUS

Popular works including biographies, commentaries, basic doctrine and Christian living.

◁◯✕ MENTOR

Books written at a level suitable for Bible College and seminary students, pastors, and other serious readers. The imprint includes commentaries, doctrinal studies, examination of current issues and church history.

◁◯✕ CHRISTIAN HERITAGE

Books representing some of the best material from the rich heritage of the church.

◁◯✕ CF4KIDS

Children's books for quality Bible teaching and for all age groups: Sunday school curriculum, puzzle and activity books; personal and family devotional titles, biographies and inspirational stories – because you are never too young to know Jesus!

Christian Focus Publications Ltd,
Geanies House, Fearn, Ross-shire,
IV20 1TW, Scotland, United Kingdom.
www.christianfocus.com